Yum!

Monica Hughes

OXFORD

Food

Do you like these foods?

orange juice
risotto
corn on
the cob

Milk

I like milk.

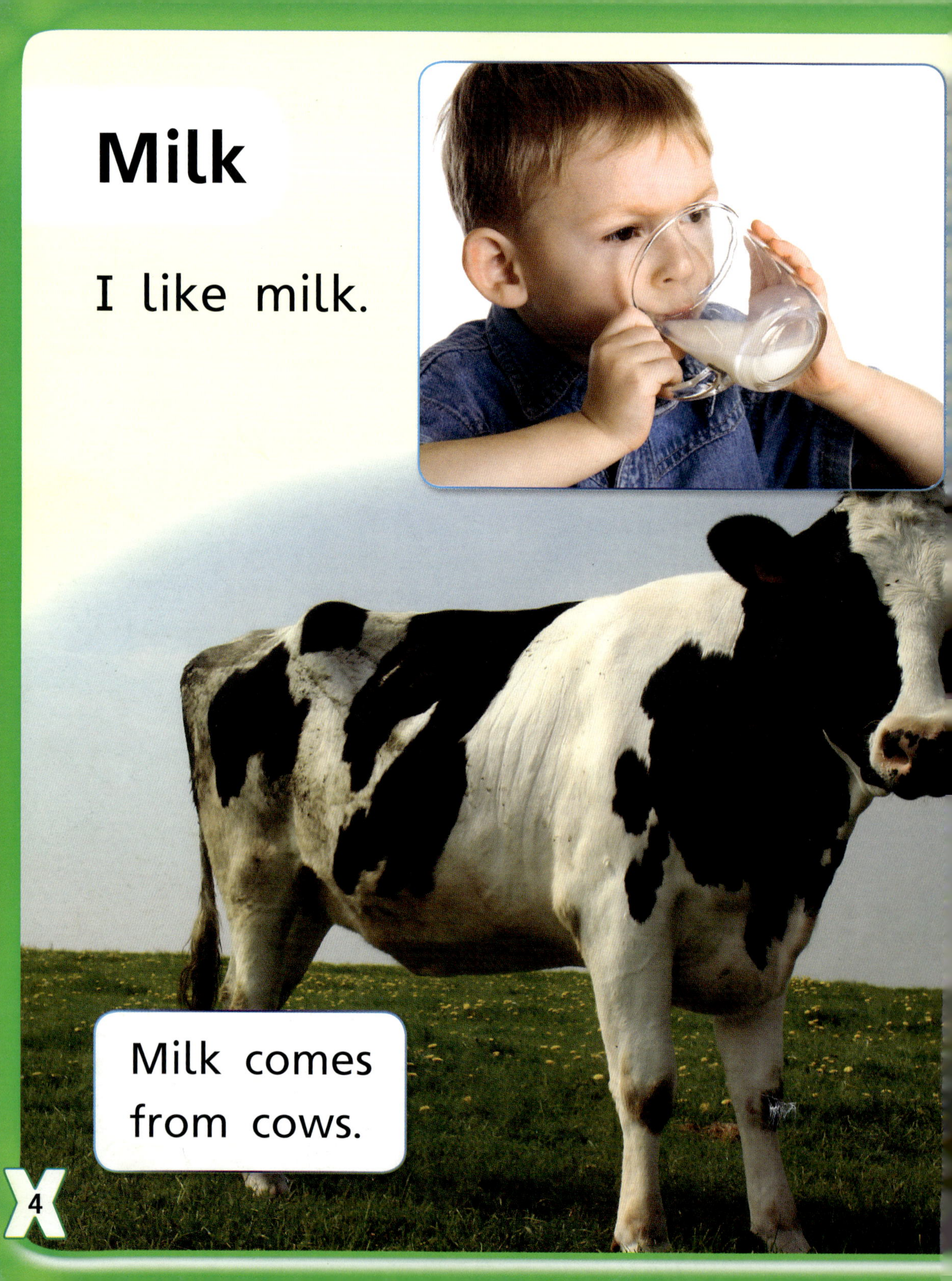

Milk comes
from cows.

What is made from milk?

Oranges

I like oranges.

Oranges grow
on trees.

What is made from oranges?

Tomatoes

I like tomatoes.

Tomatoes grow
on plants.

What is made from tomatoes?

Rice

I like rice.

Rice is a plant.

What is made from rice?

Corn

I like corn.

Corn grows
in fields.

What is made from corn?

Potatoes

I like potatoes.

Potatoes grow under
the ground.

What is made from potatoes?

What are these foods made from?